Trading Course

Ricardo Moreno

Copyright Page

Publisher: Flamenco
Release Year 2025

Index

What is Trading and How Does a Trader Make Money? 7
Find the Style That Suits You 13
Opening Your First Account 19
How a Chart Works and What is Technical Analysis 26
Repeating Patterns 34
Technical Indicators That Really Work 41
Simple and Profitable Strategies to Start Trading 48
Trading Psychology 55
How Not to Lose Your Money 61
Trading Plan 67
Your Best Tool to Improve 74
Operating Economic News and Events 80
Professional Analysis and Market Structure Theory 87
Bots, Alerts and Intelligent Systems 95
Operate with Other People's Money 102
Routines, Habits and Reality 109

What is Trading and How Does a Trader Make Money?

Imagine you're at a large fair, full of stalls where people are constantly buying and selling things. Some sell fruit, others watches, others antiques. You notice that one vendor is offering apples for $1 each, and a little further down the line another buyer is willing to pay $1.20 for that same apple. What do you do? You buy at the first stall and sell at the second. That 20-cent difference is your profit. This is how trading works, but instead of apples, you buy and sell currencies, stocks, cryptocurrencies, commodities, and other financial assets.

Trading is, basically, the art of buying something at a lower price and selling it at a higher price. It's an activity where a person, called a trader, seeks to take advantage of market movements to generate profits. The important thing is that it's not about guessing, but rather about analyzing and making intelligent decisions. Trading isn't a gamble; it's a work of observation, strategy, and emotional control.

A trader doesn't make money by being lucky. They make money when they identify an opportunity and act on a clear plan. For example, if they see that the price of the euro is rising against the dollar, they might buy euros with the idea of selling them at a higher price a few minutes, hours, or days later. If the price actually rises as expected, by selling those euros, they will have made money. That difference between the purchase price and the sale price, minus the small trading costs, is their profit.

There are many types of markets where trading is possible. The most famous is the foreign exchange market, also known as Forex, where pairs such as the euro/dollar, dollar/yen, and others are traded. There are also stock markets, where shares of companies like Apple, Amazon, and Tesla are bought and sold. Another very popular market is the cryptocurrency market, with assets like Bitcoin, Ethereum, and many more. There are also commodity markets, where you can trade gold, oil, natural gas, coffee, and others.

Each of these markets has its own dynamics, but the underlying logic is the same: buy low and sell high. Of course, that sounds easier than it is, because the price of any asset rises or falls all the time, and it does so for many reasons: economic news, political decisions, company results, or simply the behavior of supply and demand.

A trader studies these variations and looks for patterns. They use technical analysis tools, which allow them to interpret charts and predict where the price will move. They can also use fundamental analysis, which involves studying news, economic reports, company balance sheets, and other factors that influence an asset's value. Some traders use a mix of both methods.

You don't need a large amount of money to get started. Nowadays, you can start trading with a small account thanks to the leverage offered by many brokers. This means you can move more money than you actually have, allowing you to make bigger profits, but it also entails greater risks if you don't know what you're doing. Therefore, before risking real money, it's recommended to practice on demo accounts, which simulate the market without putting your capital at risk.

Trading has a great advantage: you can do it from anywhere in the world, with just a computer or cell phone and an internet connection. You don't need a boss, fixed hours, or to be in an office. But that can also be a trap if you don't take the job seriously. Because while it's true that you can make a lot of money, you can also lose it—and quickly—if you trade without knowledge or emotional control.

Money in trading doesn't appear out of thin air. It comes from other people who are trading in the same market. In other words, it's a zero-sum game: what you win, someone else loses, and vice versa. That's why it's so important to educate yourself, practice, and create a solid strategy. The successful trader isn't the smartest, but the most disciplined. The one who understands how the market works and acts without being swayed by emotions.

Trading can become a powerful source of income, even a lifestyle. But it's not magic, nor is it luck. It's a craft, and like any craft, it's learned with time, practice, and patience. The more you understand the game, the more control you have over your decisions. And in this game, whoever has control has the advantage.

So if you've ever wondered if it's possible to make money from home, with your computer, analyzing markets and making strategic decisions, the answer is yes. But it's also possible to lose everything if you do it unprepared. Trading is a tool, and like any tool, it can build or destroy. The important thing is to learn how to use it well. This book is designed to help you with just that. From the simplest to the most advanced. So that when you trade, it's not just to try your luck, but because you really know what you're doing.

Find the Style That Suits You

One of the first important decisions anyone who wants to get into trading must make is choosing a style. This has nothing to do with the clothes you wear or how you style your hair. In the trading world, style refers to how you choose to trade, the time you dedicate to it, and the pace you prefer. Not all traders are the same. Some sit in front of a screen for hours, making quick decisions. Others prefer to take their time and wait for slower, but more stable, opportunities. There is no one style that is better than another. What does exist is a style that fits you, your personality, your lifestyle, and your goals.

The first style that usually appears on the scene is scalping. This style is like running a 100-meter race. Fast, intense, and exhausting. Scalpers open and close trades in a matter of seconds or minutes. They look for small market movements and try to make many trades a day to accumulate small profits that, in the end, can add up to a significant amount. If you're a very active, impatient person who enjoys adrenaline and can make decisions in seconds without getting blocked, this may be your style. But beware: scalping is also the most demanding. It requires a fast connection, a powerful computer, and a cool head. A mistake of just a few seconds can cost you a lot of money.

The second style is day trading. This is similar to working short shifts. You trade during the day, but don't leave any trades open overnight. You start with the market and finish when it closes. You analyze, make decisions, enter, and exit within minutes or hours. It's a style that requires concentration, but it gives you a little more breathing room than scalping. You can better analyze entries, gain greater clarity on market movements, and apply more elaborate strategies. It's ideal for people who have a few hours free each day, who enjoy being in front of a screen in the mornings or afternoons, and who want complete control over what's happening while they're trading.

Then there's swing trading. This style is like hiking: you go slower, but you can cover more distance. Swing traders keep their trades open for days or even weeks. They watch the broader market movements and enter when they see a clear trend that can last. This style is perfect if you don't have time to sit in front of a screen all day. You can do your analysis once a day, place your trades with your targets and stop-losses, and then let the market do its work. It's also a style that creates less daily stress because you're not constantly watching every little price move. However, you do need patience. Sometimes it takes days for the price to reach where you expected, and during that time you have to stay calm.

And finally, we have position trading. Here we're talking about trades that can last weeks, months, or even years. This style is closer to investing than flash trading. Position traders look for really big moves, and therefore study the market with a broader perspective. They're less concerned with the small noises of everyday life. This style is for people with a more strategic mindset, who don't need immediate results and who can tolerate watching their trades go up and down without despairing. It's also useful if you have another job or can't keep an eye on the market every day.

Choosing the right style is crucial. Many traders fail because they try to trade in a way that doesn't fit their personality. For example, an anxious and rushed person trying to swing trade will suffer greatly waiting for results that take days. On the other hand, a calm and thoughtful person trying to scalp will feel pressured and make mistakes by acting too quickly. That's why knowing yourself is key. It's not just about learning strategies, but about finding a rhythm you can maintain without burning out or losing control.

Another important factor is the amount of time you have available. If you work all day, you probably can't dedicate yourself to scalping or day trading. In that case, the most logical option is to lean toward swing trading or position trading. You can analyze the market at night, when you're calm, and plan your trades calmly. On the other hand, if you have plenty of free time and enjoy constant action, you can try faster-paced trading styles. The key is for trading to fit into your life, not the other way around. Otherwise, you'll end up frustrated, stressed, or making impulsive decisions.

Don't worry if you don't choose the perfect style from the start. Many traders try several until they find the one that really works for them. The important thing is to be honest with yourself and not force a style just because someone else is making money with it. What works for someone else won't necessarily work for you. There's no one-size-fits-all formula here. There are different paths to achieving the same goal.

In this book, you'll learn tools, strategies, and methods that you can apply to any of these styles. But I advise you not to try to do everything at once. Focus. Try a style, train in it, master its rhythm and rules. And when you feel comfortable, you can adapt it, improve it, or even change it. But start with one. One that suits you, your time, your way of thinking. That's the smartest way to start, and also the surest way to make real money trading. Because the best style isn't the most famous. It's the one you can maintain with calm, consistency, and confidence.

Opening Your First Account

It's time to get your hands a little dirty. So far, we've been talking about trading from a theoretical perspective, from an idea. But for all of this to become action, you need something fundamental: open your first trading account. Without one, it's like trying to play a game without a court or ball. This account will be your gateway to the market. And don't worry, you don't need to be an expert to open one. You just need to understand what you're doing, choose wisely, and take a few concrete steps.

The first thing you should know is that you're not opening this account with a traditional bank, but rather with a specialized platform called a broker. The broker is the intermediary who connects you to the market. They receive your buy and sell orders and execute them. There are hundreds of brokers, and not all are the same. Some are reputable, with a good reputation and regulation, while others are dubious or even outright scams. Therefore, the most important step before opening your account is to choose the broker wisely.

To do this, there are a few criteria you should consider. The most important is that it's regulated. This means that the broker is accountable to an official entity that oversees it. If something goes wrong, you can file a claim. If it's not regulated, you'll be completely at its mercy. Look for brokers regulated in reputable countries like the United States, the United Kingdom, Australia, or the European Union. You can also check their website to see if they have visible licenses and registration numbers.

After that, look at what types of assets they offer. Some brokers only allow trading in stocks, others focus on currencies, others on cryptocurrencies, and many offer a mix. It depends on your chosen trading style. If you're going to trade Forex, you need a broker that gives you access to the major pairs and has good execution speed. If you're going to trade stocks or indices, make sure they have those products available. Some even allow you to trade commodities or derivatives like CFDs.

It's also important that the broker has a trading platform that's easy to use, stable, and works well on your device. The most common are MetaTrader 4, MetaTrader 5, cTrader, or even each broker's own platforms. If you're just starting out, it's ideal for the broker to give you access to a demo account. This account allows you to practice with play money, but under real market conditions. It's like a simulator. And it's one of the best places to learn without risking your money. Many brokers allow you to open a demo with just an email.

Now let's talk about the opening process itself. Once you've chosen a broker, you'll typically go to their website and see a button that says "open account" or something similar. When you click on it, they'll ask for your personal information: name, address, email, phone number, date of birth. They'll also ask you a few questions about your trading experience, your income, and your financial knowledge. This isn't meant to judge you, but because regulations require them to know who they're accepting as a client.

After completing the form, you'll be asked to verify your identity. To do this, you'll need to send a photo or scan of your ID (passport or national ID) and proof of residence, such as a utility bill or bank statement with your name and address. This part may sound tedious, but it's completely normal. Reputable brokers do this to prevent fraud and comply with international laws.

Once your account is verified, the next step is to make your first deposit. You should also pay attention here. Each broker has a different minimum. Some allow you to start with $10 or $50, others require $200 or more. If you're just starting out, don't put all your money in at once. Start with a small amount, something you're willing to lose if things don't go well. The important thing now isn't to make a lot of money, but to learn without making serious mistakes.

Deposit methods vary. Most accept credit or debit cards, bank transfers, and some also allow you to use e-wallets like Skrill, Neteller, or even cryptocurrencies. Check if there are any fees, how long it takes for the funds to be credited, and how easy it is to withdraw them afterward. Because it's not enough to deposit money; you also have to make sure you can withdraw it when you need it.

Once you have everything ready, you can start using the platform. Familiarize yourself with the environment, the buttons, the charts. Learn where everything is before making your first trade. Don't rush. Take your time to learn how it works. At this stage, using the demo account is key. Practice there as much as you want. When you feel confident, only then switch to the real account. But even then, start small. There's no rush.

Opening your account is the first step toward becoming a trader, but it's also an act of commitment to yourself. It means you stop seeing trading as a distant idea and start taking action. Like every beginning, it involves some excitement and some fear. But you're not alone. Many people have been there. The important thing is to do it calmly, judiciously, and with your feet firmly on the ground.

Remember that your account isn't a ticket to automatic wealth. It's a tool. What you do with it is up to you. If you use it well, it can help you build a new source of income, or even a new lifestyle. But if you use it unprepared, it can quickly lose you money. So don't obsess about starting with a lot of money or making a profit quickly. Right now, the most important thing is to understand how everything works. That way, when the market starts moving, you won't be improvising. You'll be ready.

How a Chart Works and What is Technical Analysis

When someone starts trading, one of the first things they see is a screen full of lines, candles, colors, moving numbers, and charts that look more complicated than an old-fashioned map. The reality is that a chart is nothing more than a visual way of showing what's happening with an asset's price. It may seem intimidating at first, but once you understand what you're seeing, everything starts to make sense. Learning to read a chart is like learning to read a language. At first, you don't understand anything, but then you can see a whole story in a single image.

A chart shows you how the price of an asset has changed over time. It could be the price of the dollar, a stock, a cryptocurrency, or any other tradable financial product. On the horizontal axis, which is the base of the chart, you see time. It can be in minutes, hours, days, weeks, or even years. On the vertical axis, you see the price. So, each point, line, or figure that appears on that chart tells you how much that asset was worth at a specific point in time.

The most popular way to display this information is with what are known as Japanese candlesticks. Each candle represents a period of time. If you're looking at an hourly candlestick chart, each candle shows you what happened to the price in that hour. If it's a daily candlestick chart, each candle summarizes an entire day. And within each candlestick are four important pieces of information: the open price, the close price, the highest price, and the lowest price reached during that time. If the candlestick is rising, it's usually green or white. If it's falling, it's usually red or black. This system allows you to see not only whether the price rose or fell, but also how it moved during that time period.

Now, understanding a chart is the first step. But to be able to make buy or sell decisions, you need to do something deeper: analyze that chart. And that's what's called technical analysis. Technical analysis is the study of charts to predict where the price might move in the future. It's not based on news, the state of the economy, or what a politician said. It's based only on the price and its past behavior. The idea behind technical analysis is simple but powerful: everything that affects the market is already reflected in the price. And if the price behaved a certain way in the past, it's likely to do so again under similar circumstances.

There are many tools within technical analysis. Some of the most common are trend lines, support lines, and resistance lines. A trend line is simply a line that connects the highest and lowest points of a price to show the general direction in which the market is moving. If prices are making higher highs and higher lows, then there is an uptrend. If they are making lower highs and lower lows, the trend is down. Drawing these lines helps you clearly see what's happening, rather than being driven by emotions or intuition.

Support is an area on the chart where the price tends to stop and bounce upward. It's like a floor. Resistance, on the other hand, is an area where the price slows down and tends to fall, as if it were hitting a ceiling. These levels are important because they show the points where many people buy or sell, generating repeated market behavior. If the price approaches a support level, it can go up. If it approaches a resistance level, it could go down. This doesn't always happen, but it happens so frequently that it's worth keeping in mind.

In addition to that, there are technical indicators. These are mathematical formulas applied to the chart to give you more information. Some measure the speed at which the price is moving, others show whether the market is overbought or oversold, and others give you entry or exit signals. The most well-known indicators are the RSI, moving averages, the MACD, and Bollinger Bands. You don't need to use them all or understand them all at once. But little by little, you'll discover which ones help you the most and how to combine them with your trading style.

A key part of technical analysis is that it's based on price action. That means the most important thing is to observe what the price is doing and not get lost in too many tools. Sometimes, the simpler, the better. Many successful traders analyze only price movement and the patterns it forms, because price tends to behave similarly in certain situations. For example, there are patterns like double tops or double bottoms, which indicate possible changes in direction. There are also formations like triangles or channels, which show you moments of consolidation and potential breakouts.

Technical analysis also helps you know when to enter, when to exit, and how much you're willing to lose if things don't go as expected. It's not just about guessing where the market is going; it's about having a plan. That's why, when you learn to read a chart and perform technical analysis, you stop acting on impulse. You start making decisions with logic, data, and strategy. And that's what separates the beginner from the professional trader.

Many people think technical analysis is some kind of magic or that you need to be a genius to understand it. But that's not the case. It's a practical, concrete, observation-based tool. The more you practice it, the more it makes sense. At first, it may seem difficult to see patterns or trends, but over time, your eye gets used to it. You begin to see order within the chaos. You start to notice that the market moves with certain patterns that repeat themselves over and over again.

Therefore, my advice is not to despair if you feel lost with charts at first. It's completely normal. Take your time to observe, to practice with a demo account, to draw lines, and to test tools. Don't try to understand everything at once. Instead, focus on understanding one thing at a time. Learn to read candles, to draw support and resistance levels, to recognize a trend. That's a good starting point. The rest will come with experience.

Technical analysis isn't a crystal ball. It doesn't predict the future with certainty. But it does give you an edge. It allows you to trade with greater clarity, more control, and more confidence. And in the world of trading, where every decision counts, that can mean the difference between making or losing money. So, consider charts your allies. They're your map on this journey. And while they may seem confusing at first, over time they become as familiar as the pages of a good book. You just have to learn to read them.

Repeating Patterns

One of the most interesting things about trading is that, although markets may seem chaotic and full of surprises, they actually behave quite predictably. How is that possible? Because markets aren't machines; they're spaces where millions of people buy and sell, and most people tend to react similarly to the same situations. This repetition in human behavior is what gives rise to the patterns that repeat on charts. And when you learn to recognize those patterns, you begin to see profit-making opportunities where you previously only saw meaningless lines and candles.

A pattern is simply a shape that price draws on the chart. That shape doesn't appear by chance. It appears because there's a constant struggle between buyers and sellers. When buyers are stronger, the price rises. When sellers dominate, the price falls. And sometimes, the market gets caught in a kind of tug-of-war between the two. It's at these moments that patterns begin to form. These patterns don't guarantee what will happen, but they give you clues. It's like seeing dark clouds in the sky. It doesn't mean it's sure to rain, but it's quite likely.

One of the most well-known patterns is the double top. Imagine that the price rises, reaches a high point, and then falls. Then it rises again to the same high point, but fails to break through, and falls again. This movement creates a sort of "M" on the chart. This is called a double top. What this pattern is telling you is that the price tried twice to break through a zone but couldn't. The sellers won the fight. And often, after this pattern, the price begins to fall sharply. This is a clear sign of weakness.

Conversely, when the price falls, rebounds, falls back to the same low, and rises again, a double bottom forms. It's like a "W." This indicates that the price tried to fall twice, but buyers defended it at the same level. It's a sign that a rise could begin. These two patterns are very easy to identify once you know them, and they appear in all markets and on all time frames. The important thing is not to desperately search for them, but to train yourself to see them clearly.

Another classic pattern is the head-and-shoulders pattern. It sounds complicated, but it isn't. It's so named because it resembles a human figure. First, the price rises and falls (that's one shoulder), then it rises higher and falls again (the head), and then it rises less than before and falls again (the second shoulder). If you draw a line through the points where the price bounced on each decline, you have what's called the neckline. When the price breaks this line, it usually falls sharply. It's a trend reversal pattern. There's also its opposite version, the inverted head-and-shoulders pattern, which heralds a possible rise.

In addition to trend reversal patterns, there are continuation patterns. These appear when the price is in a strong trend, pauses, and then continues in the same direction. An example is the triangle. Imagine the price starting to move in a narrower space, with lower highs and higher lows. It's as if the price is accumulating energy. When it breaks out of this triangle, it almost always does so in the direction it was coming from. There are ascending, descending, and symmetrical triangles. They all give you useful information about what might happen.

There are also pennants and flags. These are patterns that appear after a strong move. The price rises or falls sharply, then moves more calmly in a sloping range. This break resembles a small flag. When it breaks through this flag, it usually continues the previous move. It's as if the market takes a breath before continuing to run. These patterns are highly valued because they usually give clear signals with little risk.

In addition to the patterns formed by price movement, there are also patterns within candlesticks. For example, a candle with a small body but a long downward shadow is called a hammer. It appears after a decline and can signal a possible upward reversal. Another candle with a small body and a long upward shadow is called a hanging man, and it often appears in ceiling areas, anticipating a possible decline. These individual or combined candlestick patterns are also very useful and appear constantly if you know what to look for.

It's important to note that patterns aren't magic. They don't work 100 percent of the time. But they do have a high probability of repeating themselves and offer a statistical advantage. This means that if you use them well, with discipline and good risk management, you can make consistent profits over the long term. It's not about trading every time you see a pattern. It's about being patient and waiting for the best conditions. A pattern in a key area of the chart, accompanied by volume or confirmations from other indicators, is much more reliable than a single one.

Learning to recognize patterns is like learning to read the market's secret language. At first, it seems complicated, but over time, it begins to become second nature. Your eye becomes trained. You begin to notice that things don't happen by chance, but rather that there's a rhythm, a structure, a repetitive behavior. And when you can anticipate that behavior, your trading becomes more strategic and less impulsive.

So, spend time looking at charts. Not just to trade, but to study. See how the patterns form, what happened next, what you could have done if you'd recognized that pattern earlier. Take screenshots, make your own collections of examples, build your visual memory. Technical knowledge isn't the only thing that matters in trading, but it's certainly one of the most powerful tools you can have.

Patterns aren't a perfect get-rich-quick formula, but they are a compass. They give you direction. And when you combine them with a good plan, discipline, and emotional control, they bring you closer and closer to trading like a true professional. The market isn't as unpredictable as many people say. You just have to learn to listen to it. And patterns are one of the clearest ways the market speaks. You just have to learn to understand its language.

Technical Indicators That Really Work

One of the most common mistakes new traders make is thinking that the more technical indicators they use, the better decisions they'll make. They open a chart and fill it with colored lines, oscillators, numbers, and signals that often end up confusing more than they help. The truth is that technical indicators are useful tools, but they're not magic. They don't predict the future, they don't guarantee profits, and they certainly won't make you a professional trader just by using them. What they can do, if you understand them well and use them wisely, is give you clear signals, help you confirm what you're already seeing in the price, and increase your probability of success. The key is knowing which ones really work and how to use them without complicating things.

The first of all, and probably the most used in the trading world, is the moving average. It's a line drawn on the chart and represents the average price over a set number of candles. For example, if you use a 20-period moving average, it means that each point on that line reflects the average of the last 20 closing prices. The idea is to smooth out market movements to more clearly see where the trend is going. If the price is above the average, it usually indicates an uptrend. If it's below, it can indicate a downtrend. A very useful way to use moving averages is to combine two, one fast and one slow. For example, a 9-period and a 21-period. When the fast average crosses above the slow average, it's usually a buy signal. When it crosses downward, it can be a sell signal. It's not a perfect rule, but used judiciously, it can help you a lot.

Another indicator really worth learning is the RSI, which stands for Relative Strength Index. This indicator isn't drawn over the price, but below it, in a sort of separate window. What the RSI does is measure the strength of price movements and show you whether an asset is overbought or oversold. The value ranges from 0 to 100. When the RSI is above 70, the asset is considered overbought, which could indicate a fall soon. If it's below 30, it's said to be oversold, which could mean a rise could soon occur. But it's not about buying or selling just because the RSI crosses those zones. The idea is to combine it with what you see on the chart, with patterns, support, or resistance zones. If everything points in the same direction, the RSI can be a great ally.

A third very useful indicator is the MACD, which stands for Moving Average Convergence and Divergence. Although its name sounds complex, it's quite easy to understand in practice. This indicator is also displayed in a separate window and shows two lines crossing each other, as well as a histogram that reflects the difference between them. When the fast line crosses upwards into the slow line, it can be a buy signal. When it crosses downwards, it's a sell signal. The histogram helps you see whether this crossover is strong or not. The MACD is very good at confirming trend changes, but you have to be patient with it, as it can sometimes be too early or too late. Therefore, it's always best to use it as a confirmation, not as the sole reason for entering a trade.

One indicator that many ignore but can be very powerful is volume. Unlike the previous indicators, volume isn't a mathematical calculation of price; rather, it reflects how many trades are being made at a given time.

When you see a large candle accompanied by high volume, it means there's conviction behind that move. If the price is rising but the volume is low, that move may not have any real strength and is just a weak bounce. Volume can also warn you of potential trend changes. For example, if the price is falling and a very large green candle suddenly appears with increasing volume, strong buyers may be entering the market. Ignoring volume is like driving a car without looking in the rearview mirror. You may not need it all the time, but when you do, it can save you.

There is also an indicator called Bollinger Bands. This consists of three lines: a moving average in the center, and two bands that expand or contract depending on market volatility. When the bands are very close together, it means there is little volatility and a strong move is likely imminent. When they are very far apart, it signals that a strong move has already occurred and a pause could be imminent. Bollinger Bands can also be used to detect extremes. When the price touches the upper band, it may be overbought. If it touches the lower band, it may be oversold. But, like everything in trading, it is not a signal to act alone. It is always a good idea to look at what the price is doing at that moment and if it coincides with any important technical zones.

There are hundreds of other indicators, but you don't need all of them. In fact, the fewer you use, the better. The important thing is to understand them well. Know what they measure, how they work, and in what situations they make the most sense. A good tip is to choose two or three that you like, practice them, study them thoroughly, and see how they behave in different types of markets. For example, the RSI and MACD work well in trending markets. But in trading ranges, they may give false signals. That's where your judgment as a trader comes in. No indicator works well every time. Therefore, the best thing you can do is combine what you see in the indicators with what you see on the chart. Technical analysis always starts with the price. Indicators only come later, to confirm or reinforce what you're already observing.

In short, the technical indicators that really work aren't the newest or flashiest, but the simplest and most reliable. Those that give you clear information, that you can interpret without complications, and that you can combine with your analysis naturally. Don't turn them into useless ornaments. Don't use them as oracles either. They are tools, not absolute answers. And like any tool, their effectiveness depends on the hand that uses them. If you train your eye, if you learn to read the market and don't let yourself be carried away by emotions or hype, you'll see how these indicators help you make firmer, more confident, and, above all, more profitable decisions. That's what really matters.

Simple and Profitable Strategies to Start Trading

When you're starting out in the world of trading, it's very easy to get lost among so many strategies, methods, and systems that promise incredible results. There are videos showing magical trades, gurus claiming to have the secret formula, and forums full of people speaking in language that seems more complicated than useful. But the truth is, to get started, you don't need any of that. What you really need is a simple, clear strategy that you can understand and apply every day without racking your brains. Simplicity is not only easier to execute, but also easier to evaluate, improve, and repeat. Complexity, on the other hand, confuses you, makes you doubt, and fills you with mistakes.

A profitable strategy doesn't have to have twenty indicators or work in every possible market. It just needs to be based on clear logic and you can follow it without breaking it. One of the simplest and most effective ways to start is with a breakout strategy. This technique involves identifying areas on the chart where the price has been stalling for a while, as if the market were "accumulating" energy to make a strong move. These areas are called consolidations. When the price finally breaks through one of these zones, up or down, it usually does so with force. The trick is to wait patiently. You draw your support and resistance zones, wait for the price to approach, and when it breaks through with volume, you enter. Your stop loss is placed below or above the zone, and your target should be at least double what you risk. Simple, straightforward, and very effective if you know how to wait.

Another strategy that works well at first is bouncing off key zones. This strategy relies on finding important levels where the price has bounced before. These can be support, resistance, or even trend lines. When the price returns to one of these levels, instead of breaking through, it stops and begins to retrace. This bounce can be a good opportunity to enter a trade that follows the previous movement. For example, if the price was rising, hits a resistance, and bounces down, you can sell. If it was falling, finds a support, and bounces up, you can buy. The important thing is to wait for confirmation. Don't enter just because it touched the zone. Wait for a candle that closes in the opposite direction, a reversal pattern, or an increase in volume. This gives you more confidence that the bounce is real and not a scam.

You can also use a strategy based on moving averages. For example, a very simple and effective one is the moving average crossover. You use two moving averages, one fast and one slow, such as the 9- and 21-point moving averages. When the fast moving average crosses upward over the slow moving average, it can be a buy signal. When it crosses downward, it can be a sell signal. This strategy works best in trending markets. If the market is very sideways, it can give you false signals. That's why it's advisable to combine it with price readings. If you see the market making higher highs and higher lows, and the moving averages are also crossing upward, you have a much more reliable signal. It's a very useful strategy because it forces you to follow the trend, not go against it.

Another interesting strategy is trading trend retracements. This means you don't enter when the price has already surged, but rather wait for a small pause or pullback, and then enter with the trend. For this, you can use the Fibonacci retracement tool. You don't need to fully understand its mathematical origins. What matters is that it allows you to mark levels where the price typically stops and continues its path. For example, if the price rose sharply, you draw the Fibonacci from the beginning to the end of the movement, and it will give you levels like 38%, 50%, or 61%. Many traders look at these levels to enter when the price pulls back, because they often act as temporary support or resistance. If they are also combined with a moving average or a previous key zone, the signal is even stronger.

Finally, a very simple but powerful strategy is the false breakout. Sometimes, the price looks like it's about to break out of a zone, everyone rushes to buy or sell, and suddenly, the market turns around and does the opposite. This happens because large institutions often create false moves to trap inexperienced traders. If you learn to spot them, you can take advantage of them. For example, if the price breaks through a resistance level but immediately returns below it with a strong candle, this could be a sign that it was a false breakout. In that case, you can enter in the opposite direction, with a tight stop and a clear target. This strategy requires practice and a good reading of the price, but when it works, it usually yields very advantageous entries.

In all of these strategies, the most important thing isn't finding the one that makes the most money, but the one you understand best and can execute without hesitation. It's not about making many trades a day, but rather making the right ones. Each entry must be justified, have its reason and logic. Always have a clear plan: when you enter, where you place your stop, how much you're going to risk, and what your objective is. Without that plan, any strategy becomes a roulette wheel. With that plan, even the most basic strategy can become profitable.

Remember that no strategy always wins. All strategies have good and bad trades. What makes them profitable in the long run isn't that they always get it right, but that when they win, they win more than they lose.

That's why it's key to be disciplined, respect your rules, and not get carried away by emotion. Trading isn't about predicting the future, but rather seizing good opportunities when they arise. And if you start with simple strategies that you can master and perfect over time, you'll be much closer to making trading a stable and secure source of income. That's the goal.

Trading Psychology

Most people who start trading believe that the most important thing is knowing how to read a chart, understanding indicators, having the best strategy, or being connected to market news. But over time, they all come to the same conclusion: what really makes the difference between a trader who makes money and one who loses is psychology. That is, how you think, how you react, how you manage your emotions while trading. You can have the best strategy in the world, but if your mind isn't prepared to withstand pressure, fear, anxiety, or euphoria, you'll end up making bad decisions. It's that simple. The problem isn't the market, nor the strategy; often the real enemy is yourself.

One of the most dangerous emotions in trading is fear. Fear can cause you to close a winning trade too soon, simply because you fear the price will reverse. It can also paralyze you when entering a trade, even if everything points to a good opportunity. It can even cause you to stop trading for days after a loss that hurt more than you expected. Fear arises because you're unsure of what you're doing, or because you're risking more than you should. Therefore, a golden rule is to always trade with a risk you can tolerate without being emotionally affected. If every trade involves money that you'd hate to lose, you're going to suffer. And when you suffer, you don't think clearly. Trading becomes chaotic.

The other emotion that destroys accounts is greed. That feeling of wanting to win more, of wanting to recoup what you've lost quickly, of increasing the size of your trades to get out of trouble. That greed makes you break your own rules. Maybe your plan says you're only going to trade once a day, but after a win, you want another, and another, and you end up overtrading. Or worse, after a loss, you become enraged and make a trade without thinking it through, just to get revenge on the market. That's called trading with emotion, not reason. And those kinds of decisions, sooner or later, end badly. Greed also appears when you have a winning trade and instead of closing with a profit, you let it run uncontrolled, hoping it will turn into a fortune. Many times, that trade ends up turning around and you lose what you had already earned. Uncontrolled ambition can be just as dangerous as fear.

There's also ego. That desire to be right, to prove you know more than others, that you can predict the market better than anyone else. Ego makes you hold onto a losing trade out of pure pride, just to avoid accepting that you were wrong. Ego doesn't accept mistakes, and in trading, mistakes are part of the game. You can't always win. No one does. But if your ego won't let you accept a small loss, you'll end up enduring huge losses. A good trader doesn't seek to be right, they seek to make money. And sometimes, to win, you have to know how to lose. You have to accept when you were wrong and get out in time. That's not weakness, it's emotional intelligence.

A very important part of trading psychology is learning consistency. This means always trading with the same mindset, the same approach, without getting carried away by what happens in the moment. Because there will be days when everything seems easy, you win quickly, and everything works out. But there will also be days when nothing goes right, when the market is unpredictable and you feel frustrated. In those moments, many traders despair, change their strategy, double the size of their trades, and end up doing more damage. The right thing to do is to stay calm, review your mistakes, learn from them, and stick to your plan. Consistency doesn't come from big profits, but from doing the right thing over and over again, even when things don't go as expected.

Another key point is to have a trading routine that prepares you mentally. Before starting the day, take a few minutes to relax, review the market, and review your plan. Don't jump right into trading without clarity. A restless, stressed, or tired mind doesn't make good decisions. And after each session, take the time to evaluate what you did. Did you follow your strategy? Did you make impulsive decisions? What could you have done better? This constant self-evaluation helps you grow as a trader. Those who don't observe themselves repeat the same mistakes over and over again. And trading doesn't forgive repeated errors.

Finally, be very clear that trading is a game of probabilities. It's not about winning every time, but about winning more than you lose.

You have to think long-term. One trade doesn't define your trading career. Not even a week. What matters is the discipline with which you execute your plan, the patience with which you wait for good opportunities, and the ability to manage your emotions. Success in trading isn't just about technical knowledge; it's about the mind. Controlling your thoughts, your impulses, and your emotions is the real challenge. And if you manage to master your psychology, the market will cease to be your enemy and become your playing field. That's when everything changes.

How Not to Lose Your Money

One of the hardest but most important truths you must accept from day one in trading is this: losing money is easy. Anyone can open an account, click buy or sell, and watch their capital disappear in a matter of minutes. The difficult part—what truly requires skill, patience, and a cool head—is learning how not to lose. Before thinking about how to make money, the first thing you have to master is how to protect it. Because in this business, if you don't take care of your capital, you're out of the game. And if you're out, there's no second chance. Trading isn't a race to see who gets rich the fastest; it's a game of endurance. Whoever stays on their feet the longest wins.

The first key to not losing your money is controlling the risk on each trade. This means you should never risk more than a small percentage of your account on a single entry. Many recommend risking no more than one or two percent per trade. If you have a thousand-dollar account, for example, your maximum loss per trade should be between ten and twenty dollars. Does that seem small? Of course it is. But this isn't about winning in a single trade. It's about surviving long enough for your strategy and skills to pay off over the long term. If you risk too much and lose, you're out of ammunition. And if you're out of ammunition, there's no more battle to fight.

The second key is to always use a stop loss. Always. Without exception. The stop loss is that tool that allows you to tell the market: if the price reaches this point, I'm out. I'll accept the loss and that's it. It's your seatbelt. Not having a stop loss is like driving a car at full speed without brakes. You might get there faster, but the risk of crashing is extremely high. Many novice traders believe they can control the trade "manually," that they'll close it when they see something going wrong. But when the price goes against them and they start losing, emotions take over. Fear, denial, hope. And then they let a loss run, thinking it'll turn around, until it's too late. That's why the stop loss is non-negotiable. It protects you from yourself.

Another way to protect your money is to avoid trading without a clear reason. The market is open many hours a day, but that doesn't mean there's always a good opportunity. If you're entering just out of boredom, anxiety, or because you don't want to "miss out," you're in trouble. Every trade must have a reason. A logic. A pattern you recognize. An entry that fits your strategy. If that's not there, don't trade. Sometimes the best way to win is to do nothing. Because in trading, overtrading often leads to overlosing. Overtrading is a common trap. You feel like if you're not clicking, you're wasting your time. But in reality, you're protecting your money.

It's also important to be careful with the news. Economic announcements, central bank decisions, employment data, inflation. All of these can move the market violently. If you don't know how to interpret these news stories or lack experience, it's best to stay away during these times. Because the price can jump, go in one direction, and then change abruptly. In seconds. With no apparent logic. Trading just before or just after important news is like gambling on a roulette wheel. You might win, you might lose. But it's not trading. It's chance. And if you want to keep your money, you must avoid chance.

Another trap is increasing trade size after a loss. Many traders feel the need to recover their losses quickly, so they double their lot size, risk more, and make a more aggressive trade. This is called "revenge trading." And it's the perfect recipe for draining your account. There's nothing wrong with losing a trade. What's wrong is losing control. The right thing to do is stick to your plan. Maintain your trade size. Don't get carried away by emotion. Because if you turn one bad trade into a series of impulsive decisions, your account will bleed. And without realizing it, you'll destroy in minutes what took you weeks to build.

Finally, you must understand that in trading, losing is part of the process. No one always wins. Not even the professionals. But what separates them from the novices is that they know how to lose well. They know when to cut the trade. They know when to stay out. They know that money is guarded more than it is sought. That's why, every time you enter the market, your number one priority should be protecting your account. Because if you have capital, you have another chance. You have another play. You have a future.

Learning how not to lose money isn't the most exciting thing. But it's the most necessary. Many people want to be taught tricks, shortcuts, and magic formulas to get rich. But the truth is this: if you don't learn to conserve your money, trading will take it away from you. And it won't be the market's fault. It'll be yours. So before you look for ways to make more money, learn how to lose less. That's the foundation of everything. Without that, there's no possible path. But with that, you have a real opportunity. A chance to play the game intelligently, with discipline, and with a much better chance of winning in the long run.

Trading Plan

One of the most common mistakes most people make when they start trading is trading without a plan. They enter the market like someone entering a jungle without a map, hoping to find gold, but without knowing where they're going or how to get out if something goes wrong. They trade on intuition, impulse, or because they saw the price was rising and they don't want to be left out. But that's not how you build a trading career. That's how you build a ruin. A trading plan is your guide. Your written strategy. Your roadmap. It's what separates an impulsive beginner from a professional trader. If you really want to make money safely and consistently, you need a plan. And not a plan in your head. A real, clear, written plan. Because when you write it down, you take it seriously. And when you take it seriously, you respect yourself as a trader.

So, what should a trading plan include? To begin with, you need to clearly define what you're going to trade. Are you going to trade stocks, currencies, cryptocurrencies, indices? You can't trade everything at the same time. It's like trying to play chess and soccer at the same time. Each market has its own behavior, its own rhythm, its own rules. In your plan, you should choose your instrument. One or two at most to start. Specialize. Get to know them. Learn how they move. That gives you an advantage.

Next, your plan should specify the hours you'll be trading. It's not about sitting in front of a screen all day waiting for something to happen. That only exhausts you and leads to anxious decisions. Define a time block. Maybe you'll trade only in the morning, or only at market opening. Maybe you prefer the European or American session. But whatever you choose, make that clear in your plan. Your mind works better when it knows it has limits. And your time is just as important as your money.

Another key point of the plan is your entry strategy. Here you must detail exactly what conditions must be met for you to decide to enter a trade. What pattern are you looking for? What indicators do you use? What does the price have to do for you to say, "I'm in here"? The clearer and more specific you are, the better. It's not fair to say, "I'll get in when

I think it's going to go up." That's not a strategy. That's guessing. And guessing in trading is expensive. Your entry strategy must be logical, repeatable, and proven. If it doesn't meet those three conditions, you don't have a strategy yet.

You also have to define your exit strategy. Because it's not just about entering correctly, but also about knowing when to exit. And here there are two important exits: the loss exit and the profit exit. Where will you place your stop loss? Where will you take your profits? How will you protect your capital if the price goes against you? And how will you secure your profits if the price proves you right? These questions can't be left unanswered. They must be answered, in writing, within your plan. This prevents you from trading on emotions. It gives you structure. And that structure is what you need when your nerves betray you.

Your plan should also address money management. That is, how much you're going to risk per trade. This has to be a fixed percentage of your account, never a random figure. If you decide to risk 1 percent per trade, that's the same forever. You don't change the risk based on the mood of the day. A serious plan doesn't depend on the trader's emotional state. It's designed to operate under fixed rules. Money management is the shield that protects your account from losing streaks. Because yes, losing streaks do happen. And if you don't have clear limits, you can go bankrupt very quickly.

And there's something else that not many people mention, but that's fundamental: your plan must include your emotions. What will you do when you lose three trades in a row? What will you do if you win several times in a row and feel like you can handle anything? What will you do if you get distracted, angry, or frustrated? A good plan doesn't just talk about the market, it talks about you. Because a trader's worst enemy isn't the price, it's their own mind. It's that voice that says, "Just this once, I'll break my plan," or "I'm going to risk a little more because this one looks really good." When you listen to that voice and heed it, your account suffers. Your plan should have a protocol for those moments. Maybe stop trading if you're emotionally unstable. Or maybe a personal reminder that tells you, "The plan is more important than today's result."

Finally, your plan has to be measurable. You have to be able to review, evaluate, and improve it over time. It's not something written in stone. It's a living document. Something that grows with you. That adapts to your experience. But it's never broken. If you respect it, it protects you. If you break it, it punishes you. It's that simple.

Many people want to make money trading. And they focus on learning technical analysis, looking at charts, and watching tutorials. But what really makes the difference is having and following a plan. Because a trader without a plan is like a ship without a rudder. It can sail for a while, but sooner or later it's bound to crash. On the other hand, a trader with a plan has direction. It has direction. It has clarity. And in a world as chaotic as the market, that's worth its weight in gold.

So if you don't have a plan yet, today is the day to create one. It doesn't matter if you're still a beginner. In fact, it's better to start now. It will save you mistakes, headaches, and many unnecessary losses. Don't make it complicated. Make it simple, clear, and meaningful to you. Write it down. Read it before trading. Respect it as you would a contract with yourself. Because at its core, that's what it is: an agreement of discipline, responsibility, and a future. And that future can be bright if you learn to follow your own plan.

Your Best Tool to Improve

In the world of trading, where every click can mean a profit or a loss, many seek complex tools, automated robots, strategies that promise instant success, or secret indicators that supposedly only big banks use. But the truth is simpler than many imagine. Your best tool for improving doesn't cost money, doesn't require the internet, and can't be purchased through any course or platform. That tool is you. More specifically, your ability to observe, analyze, and learn from yourself through something as basic as keeping a trading journal.

A trading journal is your mirror. It shows you what you're doing right and, more importantly, what you're doing wrong. Writing down what you do, why you do it, and what happens after each decision you make in the market gives you a clarity you don't get any other way. In your head, everything may seem logical. You may believe you're trading with discipline, that you're following your strategy, that you're improving. But when you see it written down, black and white, with no excuses, no embellishments, you're faced with reality.

And in that reality lies the opportunity for growth.

A trading journal doesn't have to be complicated. You don't need to write pages and pages. It's enough to record a few key elements every time you trade. For example, what asset you're trading, what time frame, what your analysis was for entering, what strategy you used, how much you risked, where you placed your stop loss and take profit, what the final result was, and, above all, how you felt before, during, and after the trade. This last point, the emotional one, is often the most revealing. Because many losses don't come from technical failures, but from poorly managed emotions. And when this happens repeatedly, but you're writing it down, it becomes impossible to ignore.

At first, it may seem tedious to write down every trade. You'll wonder if it's worth it, if it's a waste of time. But over time, when you look back and review your notes, you'll find patterns that will surprise you. You'll see that you make certain decisions when you're tired, or that you make more mistakes when you break your routine. You'll notice that some strategies work better for you at certain times, or that an indicator doesn't give you as good results as you thought. These discoveries are what allow you to truly improve. It's not just about trading and trading, hoping that experience alone will make you better. It's about analyzing that experience, understanding it, and using it as a guide to correct yourself and grow.

Plus, journaling helps you reinforce what you're doing well. When you see a strategy working well for you several times in a row, it gives you confidence. And confidence, in trading, is vital. Not blind confidence, but confidence based on facts. Knowing you're acting logically and that your decisions are sound makes you stronger in the face of doubts, emotions, and market noise.

Another benefit of journaling is that it helps you stay accountable. Because when you know you're going to have to write down everything you do, you think twice before acting on impulse. You don't want to leave a record that you broke your plan, that you jumped in on a whim, or that you doubled down on an illogical bet. That pressure, no matter how small, helps you stay more focused and respect your own rules.

It's also a tool to measure your progress. Over time, you can see your progress, not only in the results, but also in your way of thinking, in how you analyze, in the quality of your decisions. And that's priceless. Because often, when we're caught up in the routine of everyday life, we don't notice how much we've improved. But when you read your notes from a month or three months ago, you realize how much you've learned. It's like looking at an old photo and seeing how you've changed.

And you don't need anything fancy to do it. You can use a notebook, a document on your computer, a spreadsheet, or even an app. The important thing is that you do it. That you take a few minutes each time you trade to write down the essentials. It's a small effort that, if made into a habit, can make a huge difference in your results.

There comes a time in every trader's life when they stop looking outside and start looking inward. That's when they truly begin to improve. And that improvement, sustained over time, is what leads to stable profitability. It's not magic. It's not luck. It's discipline, observation, and continuous learning. And the trading journal is the tool that accompanies you on that path. Not to make you perfect, but to make each day a little better than the last.

So, if you haven't already, start today. After your next trade, write down what you did, how you felt, and what you learned. Don't do it out of obligation; do it out of respect for yourself and your process. Because if you don't take yourself seriously, the market won't either. The journal isn't for others to read. It's for you. For your growth. For your success. And that success, step by step, begins to be written in your own words.

Operating Economic News and Events

One aspect of trading that many ignore at first, but that holds enormous power, is trading news and economic events. For some traders, this can be a source of great opportunities. For others, it can be a source of chaos. It all depends on how you handle it. The truth is that every week, the economic calendar releases data that shakes the markets. And if you know how to read them and act accordingly, you can take advantage of strong and rapid movements that are not seen on normal days.

Economic news is information published by governments or financial institutions that reflects the state of a country's economy. Some examples include employment data, economic growth (GDP), interest rates, inflation, central bank decisions, and other key indicators. When this data is released, markets react immediately. Sometimes they rise sharply, other times they fall sharply. But there is always movement. And where there is movement, there is opportunity.

Now, trading during the news isn't the same as trading on a quiet day. Speed changes everything here. Prices move in seconds.

Sometimes in thousandths of a second. Candlesticks on charts can jump from one price to another without passing through the intermediate points. This is called volatility, and it's what many people are looking for. But it's also what can cause you to lose money if you don't have a clear plan.

One of the keys to trading news is understanding the concept of expectations. Markets don't just react to the number released, but also to whether that number was better or worse than expected. For example, if a country is expected to create 200,000 jobs in a month, and the report says it created 300,000, that's very positive. While the number itself doesn't mean anything, the comparison with expectations is what moves the price. The same thing happens if the data is worse than anticipated. That's why it's so important to follow the economic calendar and know what to expect with each important news item.

There are several free websites where you can view the economic calendar. They show the date, the exact time of the event, the country, the type of news, the previous data, the expected data, and then, once released, the actual data. Some news has a low impact, others a medium impact, and a few have a high impact. The latter are the ones you should monitor most closely, as they are the ones that can strongly move the market. If you're trading forex, for example, interest rate decisions by the Federal Reserve in the United States, the European Central Bank, or the Bank of England can cause currency pairs to jump dozens of pips in seconds.

There are different ways to trade news. Some traders trade just before the data is released, trying to anticipate it. Others wait for the release and enter the movement after the price confirms a clear direction. Others use a technique called "strangling," where they place pending buy and sell orders before the announcement, in case the price surges in either direction. Each method has its risks and benefits, but the most important thing is not to improvise. If you're going to trade a news release, you must have a clear plan and stick to it.

Strict risk management is also essential. During important events, the market can experience "gaps," which are price jumps where intermediate levels are not respected. This means that even if you set a stop loss, it may not close exactly where you set it. The market overshoots it. Therefore, many professional traders prefer to trade news with small amounts of space to protect themselves from these unpredictable movements.

And here's another important point: not all news is the same, nor do all assets react the same way. For example, news about unemployment in the United States can affect the dollar more than the euro. Oil prices directly influence the price of crude oil, but also the currencies of producing countries like Canada. An interest rate decision in Japan moves the yen, but not as much the Australian dollar. It's key to understand which assets are connected to which news. This is learned through observation and practice.

Furthermore, it's not necessary to trade every piece of news. In fact, sometimes it's better not to. Some traders, when they see a major news story coming, simply exit the market, wait for the event to pass, and then return to trading when everything calms down. And that's not a bad thing. What matters is that you have a strategy and that you make your decisions logically, not emotionally.

Trading the news also requires mental preparation. You can't enter a high-impact event with your mind elsewhere. You have to be focused, calm, and accept that the movement can be very rapid. It's possible to win a lot in a short time, but you can also lose quickly if you're not focused. Don't get carried away with the idea of "making easy money." This isn't a lottery. It's just another tool, and like any tool, it must be used carefully.

Ultimately, using economic news and events to your advantage requires a combination of knowledge, preparation, emotional control, and experience. You don't have to become an economics expert, but you do need to learn how to interpret the basics. Enough to understand what might happen and how to react. The information is out there, free, and accessible to everyone. What makes the difference is how you use it.

So my advice is this: start by observing. Don't trade yet. See how the market reacts to certain news. Note what happens. Learn how the asset you're trading moves at that moment. When you have enough information and feel ready, create a strategy. And then, cautiously, start trading. Always with risk management. Always with respect for the market. Because news doesn't forgive those who improvise. But it does reward those who prepare.

Professional Analysis and Market Structure Theory

Once you've understood how charts, indicators, and even news stories work, it's time to take a deeper step: thinking like a pro. And to do that, you have to understand market structure. This is where many novice traders fail because they stay on the surface, believing that a moving average or a candlestick pattern alone will make them money consistently. But professional traders don't trade like that. They see the market differently. They observe how the overall price structure moves. They see what's behind the movements. And that's what I'm going to teach you in this chapter.

Market structure theory is based on a very simple but powerful idea: price moves in cycles. Always. On all time frames. It doesn't matter if you're looking at a one-minute chart or a monthly chart. Price always repeats the same logic. That logic can be roughly divided into three phases: the accumulation phase, the expansion phase (or trend), and the distribution phase. Then it starts again. This cyclical pattern is what many call market structure.

Imagine for a moment a tide in the sea. First it rises, then it falls, and then it rises again. That's how prices work too. But unlike the sea, here it's human decisions, emotions, and large capital that make it happen. Therefore, when you learn to identify these phases, you can anticipate many movements and avoid falling into the traps the market constantly sets.

Accumulation is the first phase. It's when the price moves in a narrow, sideways range, without much clear direction. This is where professional traders are quietly buying, unnoticed. There aren't any big moves, but they're slowly getting in. Meanwhile, most retail traders are bored, think nothing's happening, and sometimes even sell. But the professionals are loading up their positions for what comes next. This phase usually appears after a big drop, when everyone is scared and thinks the market will continue to fall. Right there, the big players are buying.

Next comes the expansion or trend phase. This is when the price finally decides to move strongly in one direction. It can be up or down, but the important thing is that it has already broken out of the range. This is the most profitable phase if you know how to enter. And it's the one that excites traders the most because there is movement, there is strength, there are opportunities. At this point, many retail traders are just starting to buy, when the movement is already well underway. But professionals were already in before, during the accumulation. That's why their position is much safer and more profitable.

Then, when the movement has already covered a good stretch, distribution arrives. It's a phase similar to accumulation, but it occurs at the top. The price moves within a range again. There are no clear breakthroughs. It's a period of uncertainty. This is where professionals begin to sell what they bought earlier. But they do so slowly, intelligently. Meanwhile, retailers continue buying because they believe the price will continue to rise. And when the market is already heavily loaded with poorly placed purchases, the fall comes. And the cycle repeats itself.

Understanding this structure gives you a huge advantage. Because you no longer trade on impulse or what seems like it. You begin to read the market as a story. A story that tells you who's buying, who's selling, where the novices are trapped, and where you could position yourself with logic and strategy. It's like looking at a chessboard and knowing that every move has a purpose, not a coincidence.

Another fundamental part of professional analysis is identifying relevant highs and lows. In an uptrend, the price creates increasingly higher highs and increasingly higher lows. This means the structure remains bullish. But when the price fails to make a new high, or breaks a previous low, this is a warning sign. A distribution or even a trend reversal could be beginning. This reading is more powerful than any indicator because it doesn't rely on mathematical calculations, but rather on observing actual price behavior.

Furthermore, professionals pay close attention to liquidity levels. What does this mean? In simple terms, they are areas where the market has left traces of interest: areas where many people have placed orders, either buy or sell. These areas are usually close to previous highs and lows. Large market participants know this, and they often make rapid moves toward these areas to capture the liquidity there. It's as if they were fishing in a place where they already know there are fish.

Another key concept is market traps. These occur when the price appears to be breaking through an important level, but in reality it's just generating a false breakout. Many retail traders enter at this point, believing they're trading a clear signal, but end up trapped. The price turns sharply, leaving them with a loss. Professionals know how to spot these traps and often trade against the grain. They don't follow the herd. They analyze with a cool head.

It's also important for you to understand that professional analysis isn't a set of fixed rules. It's a way of thinking. It's about observing what's happening and asking yourself: Who's winning here? Who's losing? What's the likelihood that the price will continue or reverse course soon? Am I entering at a good time or am I just getting carried away by the emotion of the movement? These questions move you away from impulse and toward a strategic mindset.

To put this theory into practice, I recommend looking at the chart on different time frames. Don't just stick to the one-minute or five-minute time frame. Look at the one-hour, four-hour, even the daily. That's where the overall structure is best seen. And then you can fine-tune your entry on lower time frames. But if you don't know what part of the cycle you're in, any trade can become a gamble.

Finally, remember that market structure isn't a magic formula. It's not infallible. But it is a solid, logical, and professional way to understand how prices move. It's the foundation upon which all serious trading strategies are based. And if you learn it well, you'll stop chasing magic indicators and start building a market vision that actually works.

This type of analysis will make you see the market through different eyes. Clearer. More objective. And above all, more profitable. Because where others see confusion, you'll begin to see patterns. Where others see chance, you'll see logic. And where others lose money because they don't understand what's happening, you'll rest easy knowing you're one of those who truly understand how this game works.

Bots, Alerts and Intelligent Systems

When you're starting out in the world of trading, the most common approach is manual trading. You sit in front of the chart, wait for a signal, decide whether to enter or exit, and do everything yourself. This stage is great for learning because it forces you to be attentive and make decisions based on your own judgment. But as you gain experience and better understand how the market behaves, you realize something very important: you can't be glued to the screen all day. And that's where bots, alerts, and smart systems come in. They're not magic or shortcuts to making easy money, but they can become very powerful tools if you use them intelligently.

Let's start with bots. A trading bot is a program that executes trades automatically, following the rules you specify. In other words, it's like an assistant that works for you, but without emotions, fatigue, or distractions. You teach it a strategy, set the parameters, and it takes care of searching for opportunities, opening trades, setting stop losses, taking profits, and closing them when appropriate. There are very simple bots and others that are extremely complex. Some work within platforms like MetaTrader or TradingView, and others are proprietary developments with proprietary technology. The important thing to understand is that a bot is only as good as the strategy behind it. If your strategy is bad, the bot will trade poorly. If your strategy is solid, the bot can help you execute it without errors.

Using a bot doesn't mean you stop trading. It means you stop doing it manually all the time. You're still the one designing, testing, optimizing, and adjusting the strategy. The bot only executes it. But the real decision remains in your hands. This allows you to have more free time, avoid emotional mistakes, and execute more precisely. It's also useful for trading during times when you might not be awake or available, such as in the early morning or during your workday.

Now let's talk about alerts. Alerts are automatic signals that notify you when something you're expecting happens on the chart. For example, you can set an alert to notify you when the price crosses a line, when it reaches a support level, when an indicator gives a signal, or when a certain volume condition is met. Alerts don't operate for you, but they do help you avoid missing important opportunities. Imagine you're at the supermarket or at work, and suddenly an alert sounds on your phone telling you: "The price reached the level you were expecting." This allows you to open your platform and take action in time. Alerts reduce the stress of staring at the chart all day. They give you freedom and control at the same time.

There are platforms that allow you to program alerts very easily. TradingView, for example, has a comprehensive alert system that you can connect to your email, your phone, or even automated bots using external tools. This allows you to have a kind of virtual assistant that notifies you only when it's really worth looking at the screen.

Finally, smart systems combine the best of bots and alerts. These are platforms that not only execute strategies, but also learn, adjust, or combine multiple complex conditions to operate in a more refined manner. Some use artificial intelligence, machine learning, or conditional rules that allow decisions to be adapted according to the market context. Although this sounds advanced, it is becoming more accessible to individual traders. You no longer need to be a programmer to access these tools. There are interfaces that allow you to build your own system visually, as if putting together a puzzle, without writing a single line of code.

Of course, it's important to be clear: no system, no matter how intelligent, replaces your judgment. All these resources are there to help you, not replace you. You are responsible for what happens. You define when to activate a bot, when to disable it, when to trust an alert, or when to intervene manually. If you blindly trust a machine, without supervision or judgment, you'll lose money sooner or later. But if you understand how to use these tools strategically, they can become a true ally in taking your trading to the next level.

A great advantage of working with bots or alerts is that they force you to be organized. If you want a machine to understand your strategy, you first have to have a clear strategy. You can't trade "by eye." You have to define specific rules: when you enter, when you exit, how you calculate your risk, under what conditions you decide not to trade. This clarity is essential for any system to work. And in the process of creating a bot or programming an alert, you force yourself to refine your ideas. To think logically. To backtest. And that, in itself, greatly improves your level as a trader.

It's also important to test everything before trading with real money. If you design a bot, run it in demo mode first. If you set up alerts, test them in the real market without trading, just to see if they work as expected. This saves you trouble. It gives you time to fine-tune details. And it allows you to correct errors you wouldn't see if you were just doing it in your head.

To close this chapter, I want you to be clear about one thing: using bots, alerts, or smart systems isn't a sign of weakness. On the contrary, it's a sign of maturity as a trader. It means you understand your limits, respect your time, and are willing to rely on tools that make you more efficient. But always with your head on straight. Always with control in your hands. Because in the end, true intelligence lies within you. Machines only do what you teach them. So, if you want them to trade well, first make sure you're the one doing the right thinking. And when that happens, these tools can take you much further than you thought possible.

Operate with Other People's Money

One of the most powerful, yet least understood ideas in the trading world is that you don't need a lot of your own money to make good money. In fact, many successful traders started without much capital, but they understood something key from the start: you can trade with other people's money. I'm not talking about borrowing money from a friend or going into debt with the bank. I'm talking about something much smarter, legal, professional, and accessible: third-party investment capital. There are people, companies, and platforms willing to give you money to trade the market if you prove you know how to do it. And you get to keep a share of the profits. It's that simple.

This is called funded trading or prop trading. Prop comes from "proprietary." A proprietary trading firm gives you access to trade with their money in exchange for a share of the profits. It's a win-win model: they have traders who trade for them without risk to the company, and you have access to capital without putting up your own. But, of course, they're not just going to give you the money. First, they want to make sure you know what you're doing. For that, there are tests.

Simulators. Assessments. They ask you to trade on a demo account with clear rules: you can't lose more than a certain percentage, you must reach a certain profit, you must have proper risk management. If you achieve this, they approve you. And if you do well, they fund you.

This opens a huge door for any trader who doesn't have a lot of money. Let's say you only have $200, and you know that's not enough to make a living from trading. But if you demonstrate in an evaluation that you can turn a virtual $10,000 account into $11,000 with good discipline, without taking too much risk, then a firm can give you a real account of $10,000, $25,000, or even $100,000 to trade. You don't put a penny out of your pocket. You just apply your knowledge and skills. And if you make a profit, they share it with you. In most cases, you keep between 70% and 90% of what you earn. The rest goes to them. It's a fair deal.

There are many platforms that offer this type of service. Some are internationally renowned, with thousands of traders worldwide. Others are newer, with different conditions. But the mechanism is the same: they evaluate your capabilities, approve you if you meet expectations, and then give you a real account to trade with their money. This isn't an easy shortcut. The tests are often demanding. You have to be consistent, not overtrade, respect the rules, and stay calm. But if you've already been training with a demo account, if you've already polished your strategy, and if you understand how to control your emotions, you're ready to try.

Furthermore, trading with other people's money has a very important mental benefit. It forces you to take it seriously. You're no longer playing around. You're no longer trying things out for the sake of trying. You're trading responsibly, because you know there's a company behind that account that trusts you. That changes the way you act. It makes you more professional. And at the same time, it protects you from the fear of losing your own capital, which sometimes paralyzes novice traders.

Another detail that many people don't know is that you can also get private investors. People who know your results, trust you, and give you capital to trade. This doesn't happen overnight, but over time, if you build a solid track record, you can attract partners or clients who tell you: I'll put up the money, you trade, and we'll share what we earn. That's why it's so important to keep professional records of your trading. A journal, statistics, screenshots, clear results. That's your resume as a trader. And if it's done well, it's worth more than any college degree.

There are even platforms that allow you to automate this process. You can connect your account to services that display your results in real time, where other users can see how you trade, copy you, or hire you as a manager. This not only gives you visibility, it can also become a steady source of income. But it all starts the same way: with discipline, practice, and the firm determination to do it right from the start.

There are those who despise other people's money because they believe it makes them dependent. But it's just the opposite. Using other people's capital gives you financial freedom without putting you at risk. It allows you to scale faster. It allows you to make a living from trading without having to save for years to build significant capital. And it connects you to a network of opportunities that previously seemed distant. Of course, you have to do it wisely. Read the terms and conditions of each company. Understand the risks. Avoid false promises. But if you choose well, prepare seriously, and respect the process, you can build a career as a funded trader.

The key is to think like a pro from today. It doesn't matter if you're trading with a demo account or a $50 account. Act as if you're managing a large account. Control your risk. Be patient. Evaluate your mistakes. Adjust your strategy. All of this prepares you for that moment when someone says: I trust you, here's my capital, grow it. That moment comes for those who take it seriously. And when it comes, it changes your life.

So don't wait until you have a lot of money to think big. Think big now, and be prepared. Because if you do it right, it won't be your account that will grow, but your ability to multiply other people's money and keep a portion of the profits. That's a real way to make safe money trading, without the risk falling entirely on your shoulders. And the best part is, you're not dreaming about something far away. It's already happening. You just need to be ready to take advantage of it.

Routines, Habits and Reality

One of the most common mistakes people make when they start trading is believing that everything depends on the strategy. That if you find a good combination of indicators, a perfect pattern, or a robot that works, it's all solved. But the truth, and I can tell you this with all my real-world experience, is that profitable trading isn't sustained by technique alone. It's sustained by habits, routines, and an organized way of living and thinking every day. It doesn't sound as exciting as finding the magic formula, but it's a thousand times more important. Because if you don't have solid habits, you can have the best strategy on the planet and still lose everything.

Trading is like a professional sport. And you're the athlete. It doesn't matter if you play tennis well if you never practice, if you sleep poorly, if you eat junk food, if you get angry every time you lose a point. That's how the market works. It's not enough to know; you have to be prepared. And that preparation starts with your daily routines. There's no one-size-fits-all formula, but there are certain basic principles you must understand and apply, no matter what, if you want to survive and thrive as a trader.

First, there's the mental routine. Every day, before opening a trade, you have to have your head in the right place. You can't trade well if you're angry, tired, anxious, or distracted. That's why many successful traders have small rituals before starting: they meditate, write down their goals, and check in with their emotions. It's not witchcraft, it's mental hygiene. Just like you wash your face or brush your teeth, you need to cleanse your mind before facing the market. Because the market is going to test you, it's going to shake the world around you, and if you're not on your best footing, you're going to fall.

Next comes the technical routine. Before trading, review the economic calendar, analyze the day's important levels, mark your entry and exit zones, and have a clear plan. Don't enter on impulse. Don't be guided by what others say. Take time every day to prepare for your session. Like a surgeon checking his instruments before operating.

Don't improvise. Because in trading, improvisation is expensive.

Another key routine is rest. Many people obsess over staring at the chart all day, as if that would yield better results. But the human brain has limits. You can't spend eight hours in front of a screen making high-pressure decisions without burning out. You're not a machine. You need breaks. You need time to disconnect, to recharge, to avoid burning out. Because if you burn out, you'll trade badly. You'll make desperate decisions. And there's no turning back. The market doesn't forgive mental fatigue.

There are also habits outside of trading. Sleeping well, eating healthy, moving around a bit. All of these directly influence your performance as a trader. It sounds exaggerated, but it isn't. A bad night's sleep can lead to impulsive trading the next day. A heavy meal can make you lose focus at the key moment. Your body and mind are connected, and if one part isn't working, neither will the other.

And then there's the hardest part to accept: reality. The reality that you're not going to win every day. The reality that sometimes you're going to lose, even if you do everything right. The reality that progress is slow, that you're not going to make a living from trading in a week, or a month, or maybe not even a year. This is the part many don't want to see. But it's essential. Because if you buy into the fantasy that you're going to get rich quick, you're going to make bad decisions. You're going to over-risk, you're going to over-trade, you're going to get frustrated. And that's going to make you give up.

The reality is also that trading can be boring. Yes, you read that right. It's not always adrenaline. It's not always excitement. Often it's waiting. It's doing nothing. It's repeating the same steps every day. And that's where discipline comes in. Because anyone can trade with excitement for a couple of days. But staying steadfast, patient, and repetitive over weeks and months—that's what builds a real trader. Not one who seeks action. One who seeks consistency.

Therefore, beyond strategies, you have to build a life around trading. An organized life, with structure, with limits. Have a time to start and a time to end. Have scheduled breaks. Have clear goals. Keep a record of your trades. Have time to review, learn, and correct. All of this isn't optional. It's part of the job. And the sooner you understand this, the faster you'll progress.

In the end, the traders who consistently make money aren't the smartest, the fastest, or the ones who know every indicator in the world. They're the ones who have solid routines, work habits, and maturely accept the reality of trading. Those who understand that it's a process. That success doesn't come from one winning trade, but from hundreds of small decisions made correctly every day.

So if you're just starting out, don't obsess over technique alone. Start building your routines today. Your tomorrow begins with what you do today without anyone asking you to. And if you do it right, over time, the results will come. Not because you're lucky. But because you've made trading a serious, responsible, and consistent lifestyle. That's the true foundation of success in this world. And that, although it may seem invisible, is what separates the amateurs from the professionals.

www.ingramcontent.com/pod-product-compliance
Lightning Source LLC
LaVergne TN
LVHW090419210926
848480LV00002B/626